CROWN

A Year in the life of the Queen Mother

IAN LLOYD

JEWEL

CROWN JEWEL

A Year in the life of the Queen Mother

IAN LLOYD

BLOOMSBURY

FOR MY PARENTS, RAYMOND AND IRENE LLOYD

First published in Great Britain 1989
Bloomsbury Publishing Limited, 2 Soho Square, London W1V 5DE

A CIP catalogue record for this book
is available from the British Library

ISBN 0–7475–0494–6

Art direction by Simon Jennings
Designed by Simon Jennings and Alan Marshall, Inklink
Typeset by Bookworm Typesetting, Manchester
Printed in Spain by Gráficas Estella, SA

Contents

Introduction

IT HAS SOMETIMES *been claimed that the woman we dream about most is the Queen, the ultimate status symbol. In my case, however, it is Her Majesty Queen Elizabeth the Queen Mother. I use the word 'dream' loosely, since a few of my dreams have been nightmares. One recurs in which thousands of Queen Mothers march down a never-ending red carpet while I tearfully try to load film into my camera. Another has featured me coming across Her Majesty sitting alone in the middle of a cornfield, sketching. Breaking all the rules of etiquette, I asked her to stay there for as long as she could while I ran off to try to find the camera. Bizarre dreams in which the Queen Mother carries her plastic chair out of the Royal Variety Performance while kicking her legs to 'The Lambeth Walk' are also part of my night-time world.*

Perhaps this obsession has finally pushed me over the edge. Certainly the Oxford camera dealer who sold me the equipment in the first place thinks me odd. Having shown me half a dozen cameras capable of photographing stampeding elephants at six paces, or a daisy two miles away, he seemed put out when I told him the reason for the purchase. 'Well, you're the first person I've met who's buying £1,000 worth of camera equipment to photograph the Queen Mother.' People say that I am mad, stupid or plain simple. Others are curious or amazed, and some become excited, demanding the latest update on royal fashion or a juicy, no-holds-barred revelation.

Although I am sure that there is nothing to link photographing the Royal Family with mental disturbance, those fanatics who, like me, travel the length of the country to snap a visiting royal certainly show signs of a Jekyll-and-Hyde split. For five days of the week, my life placidly ticks over in the history department of Oxford's largest bookshop. Besides selling history books I act as a resident guru, being expected to know the details of all royal visits west of London and to be able to explain to American tourists why Princess Michael has the same name as her husband.

All my leisure time is carefully planned to fit in with the Queen Mother's engagements, which are announced beforehand by Clarence House and printed in several magazines devoted to royalty, as well as in The Times *and the* Daily Telegraph. *On the day of the engagement I check the time of arrival in either of those newspapers, cycle madly through Oxford to the station, throw my bike in the guard's van and set off for London, where I pedal to wherever the visit is taking place. Should I be stranded in the capital after a late-night engagement, I stay in Tooting with Louisa, my closest and longest-suffering friend. Louisa keeps in her fridge a permanent stock of professional film cooled to the right temperature, and is no longer surprised to be given the occasional bunch of red roses that the Queen Mother has failed to spot me holding when she is on a walkabout.*

HOW IT ALL STARTED

My photographic interest in the Queen Mother dates back to the late 1970s, when I produced eight blurred shots of Her Majesty on a walkabout. They were all lovingly enlarged and sent to Clarence House, where a lady-in-waiting bravely deemed them 'excellent'. From then on, I was under the spell, set on the royal road that has led me on hundreds of occasions to the very portals of the House of Windsor.

One way or another the image of the Queen Mother has become an integral part of my life. As I look back, memories vie for prominence; times such as Ascot in 1988 when she greeted me with 'Nice to see you' as her carriage drove past. Two years earlier she gave me a smile of recognition at a service in Westminster Abbey to mark the 900th anniversary of the Domesday Book. Years before that, in the late 1970s, after a particularly soaking session in London, I received a note that concluded, 'Queen Elizabeth hopes that you didn't get too wet standing in the rain outside Clarence House,' following her visit to Brixton.

The most unlikely moment in all this time was perhaps the day I carried home on the bus a life-sized cardboard cut-out of the Queen Mother that had been used by the Oxford branch of the Halifax Building Society for a window display, and which now waves at me from across the living room.

Who are the other mad fools, if any, who are desperate enough to spend hours waiting around to photograph a royal appearance? There is a core of about ten of us who patrol central London on the look-out for a Rolls-Royce, tiara, corgi or any other sign of an imminent royal visit. There is our own 'Queen Mother', Ivy, a retired hospital secretary from Wood Green who, just over five feet tall, has been able to rely on her frailty to work her way to the front of any crowd since VE Day. 'The Queen' is probably Judith, who is a station supervisor for London Transport and has been photographing the Royal Family since she arrived from Australia in 1973. Those years of dedicated photography have been rewarded by occasional gifts from the Duke and Duchess of Gloucester, convivial chats with Princess Margaret, and one supreme accolade: several years ago Princess Alice used one of her photographs as the portrait design for her Christmas card. Judith is known by every royal chauffeur, each of the twenty-four Royal Protection officers and half the police in central London.

Julia, in her mid-twenties, is our token Duchess of York. She commutes from Horsham in West Sussex to a London insurance office, and last year waited on and off for seventy-two hours outside the Portland Hospital for the birth of Princess Beatrice. She travels the length and breadth of the country photographing Princess Alexandra, who has been known to shout, 'Hello Julia, how's your mother?' while accompanying a surprised mayor down a red carpet.

Then there is Mark – 'Prince Charles', since he lives in the Duchy of Cornwall – whose favourite royal is Princess Alice; Peter and Harry, two brothers from north Surrey, both civil servants; Fraser, a bookseller from Windsor; and, finally, Gill, whose mother once smuggled me, as her 'grandson', into a photo session after the 'Children of Courage' ceremony at Westminster Abbey.

Each of us has at least ten years' experience of photographing the Royal Family. Thousands of miles of road and film have flashed by, as well as countless evenings, holidays and 'diplomatic illnesses' in an insatiable desire to witness day-to-day royal events. The drawbacks are many. Few people other than professional photographers would have been willing to wait the ten hours that we stood outside Clarence House on the Queen Mother's birthday. Getting a clear view of the Royal Family at the Braemar Games can involve a six-hour wait, and even winter engagements such as the Remembrance Day appearance at the Cenotaph and the Royal Variety Performance normally entail at least four hours of being crushed against a safety barrier. Moreover, travelling to Balmoral or Sandringham by public transport, while carrying cameras and perhaps a ladder for better viewing, in itself rivals any Outward Bound course.

On the other hand, the benefits of amateur status can be immeasurable. Besides the thrill of sometimes being recognized by the Royal Family, there are the rare occasions when a royal pose is offered. For instance, while visiting Edinburgh, the Queen stopped in front of Mike, a caterer from Glasgow, and said, 'Well, I'd better smile for you!' before adjusting her collar for the picture. In addition, there are unexpected treats, such as the time in 1987 when the Duchess of Gloucester sent tickets for eight of us to stand in the forecourt of Buckingham Palace to witness the arrival of King Fahd of Saudi Arabia.

Although none of the group would ever do anything to compromise or embarrass the Royal Family, it is nevertheless fun to use the knowledge we have gained over the years to spot the Queen and her family off-duty or on semi-private engagements. We recognize the security officers, staff and friends, and we know which weddings, memorial services and first nights the royals are likely to attend. Being able to identify all the royal cars is itself an advantage: in Oxford alone it has led to my spotting Princess Anne shopping in a delicatessen, the Duchess of Kent visiting Trinity College, and the Princess of Wales having lunch after attending her brother's graduation. There have been red herrings too, however, especially when Harold Macmillan, the late Chancellor of the university, used to sweep past in his Rolls-Royce to dine at Balliol.

Some amateur photographers are probably more experienced in covering royal visits than the police on duty. Many a fresh-faced constable, having asked us, 'Who's here then?' has been crushed by Judith's retort: 'Well if you don't know who you're protecting, we're not going to tell you!' At the 1984 Chelsea Flower Show I even had to chase after the sergeant who had gone off duty after carefully locking up the side entrance following the Queen's visit. He had not realized that Princess Alexandra and Princess Michael of Kent were both still inside. And three years later, the police had all left when the Queen Mother's car, on its way from Butchers Hall, became trapped between two parked cars, and three of us had to guide it through, much to Her Majesty's delight.

On one occasion we averted by chance a potential fiasco. The Duchess of Gloucester drove past a few of us who were standing outside the Royal College of Physicians as she headed for the Royal College of Surgeons and, recognizing Judith, asked her chauffeur which member of the Royal Family we were all waiting for. We never found out whether it was Her Royal Highness or her driver who suddenly realized the almighty error first, but the Rolls-Royce and its escort did an emergency U-turn and the Duchess, slightly later than planned, duly arrived to visit the physicians – rather than the surgeons.

From time to time, one or other of us has been asked to take photographs of a specific public or private engagement: from Princess Alice attending a reception off the Brompton Road to the Kents visiting Mansion House. Some venues fail to arrange for photographers to document the event. For instance, after the Queen's visit to the Royal Caledonian Club two years ago, several of us were approached by the Royalty Protection squad to send in our photographs.

The Royal Family offers friendliness, though never friendship, and provided none of us oversteps the fine line dividing the two – as did the agency photographer who took the Duchess of Gloucester by the arm and asked her to look in the direction of his colleagues – we can benefit from royal patronage and just very occasionally, if it is raining hard, receive a lift to the tube station from the Duke of Gloucester's chauffeur or Princess Margaret's.

THE QUEEN MOTHER AND PHOTOGRAPHERS

Although 'royal-watchers' come and go, the London-based group will battle against every type of illness, financial crisis and Arctic weather to photograph its favourite member of the Royal Family – the Queen Mother.

Why the Queen Mother? Because she is dedicated and hard-working (in 1988 she fulfilled 120 engagements). She is evidently concerned to see, and be seen by, ordinary people as well as civic dignitaries, and above all, she proves that at eighty-nine life can be terrific fun. The Queen Mother is quite simply brilliant to photograph. Whether the camera belongs to a seasoned photographer or to a six-year-old Brownie, its owner is never disappointed. If they are, it can never be put down to the Queen Mother's being unco-operative. She is the only member of the Royal Family who appears truly unconcerned by the invasion of the paparazzi (at least fifty of them followed her around the Royal Smithfield Show in 1988), or by the intrusion of boom-mikes and the latest photographic equipment. Finding her way impeded by a 500-mm lens on a tripod at Egham in May, she touched the end of it, saying, 'Dear me, that looks rather frightening.'

The Queen Mother nearly always greets photographers with a polite 'Good morning'. When she steps out of a car, she looks towards both sides of the crowd to make sure that everyone can see her and photograph her. Then there is the final glance over her shoulder as she enters the building she is visiting. This usually catches out the novice photographer.

I once overheard the Queen Mother say of the press, 'Well, they have to get

their pictures or nobody will know that I've been here, will they?' She also appreciates the fact that a photographer, whether amateur or professional, may have waited up to five or six hours to see her. And she knows what makes a good picture. For instance, when she visited the Royal Windsor Flower Show in July 1987, and a gust of wind blew the vicar's hat off just as he bowed in her direction, she roared with delight and shouted over to us, 'I hope you photographed that!'

This spirit of co-operation was again evident the following year when the Queen Mother opened a police convalescence home in Goring-on-Thames, Oxfordshire. During the visit she was presented with a wooden bench for the gardens of Royal Lodge. All the photographers were tacitly imploring her to sit on it. The Queen Mother looked at us and then at the bench. 'Shall I sit on it?' A swift chorus of 'Yes please, Ma'am' followed, and then she was surrounded by the whirr of a mass of cameras.

That same year the Queen Mother visited the Downtown project, the docklands redevelopment scheme in and around Bermondsey, in South London. Her Majesty made a poignant speech recalling her previous visits during the Blitz. Behind her, as a brilliant imaginative gesture, two thirty-foot photographs showed the then Queen Elizabeth and King George VI making one of these very visits. Again, she asked us whether or not we wanted her to pose in front of them, and to universal thanks she obligingly stood against a wall of sandbags and smiled up at her own image.

Knowing where she expects the photographers to be, the Queen Mother also knows where she wants them to be. She knows how to make sure that we see her, even if, as at St Paul's Cathedral in July 1988, she has to stand on tiptoe to wave at us over the heads of choirboys. Similarly she will edge round officials without taking her eyes off them or appearing discourteous. At Scrabster, on the north coast of Scotland, that August, she walked into the middle of a puddle rather than ask the Lord Lieutenant to move.

Her Majesty gently guides those officials who are oblivious of the needs of the press. For instance, at a tree-planting ceremony in November in the grounds of Chelsea Hospital, she was completely obscured by her excited host. In response to our plaintive chorus of 'Ma'am, Ma'am', she suggested to the gentleman that he 'may possibly be in the way'.

If the photographer has completely botched the opportunities, there is always the possibility of last-minute royal help. The Queen Mother saw me fail to find a good place to photograph her arrival at St Nicholas's Church, King's Lynn for a concert given in her honour by Rostropovich. She delayed her entrance at the church door, saying, 'I don't think you got that, did you?' before giving a special pose in my direction. Similarly at the Royal Smithfield Show in December, she obligingly helped a trainee photographer who shocked officials by asking her to move forward so that he could photograph her with her own prize-winning heifer.

I was advised by a member of the royal household never to underestimate the Queen Mother on, for instance, her knowledge of cameras and their use. I had the opportunity to verify this in December when I was photographing Her Majesty at a lunch engagement in the City. Amused by the constant blitz of the flash-gun, she said, 'Flash, click, click, what a lot of noise! Incidentally, what type of camera is it?' Like thousands before me in the same situation, I went totally blank, and fumbled with the camera to find its make. 'Er, it's a Canon, Your Majesty.' 'Ah Canon,' came the swift reply, 'that's Japanese, isn't it?'

Her Majesty knows whether the photographer should be using 100 or 400 ASA film. She understands the difficulties of photographing through glass, and lowers her car window as she leaves each engagement. She is also adept at dealing with flash photography. When the Vice-President of Sandringham Women's Institute asked her how she and the Queen coped with constant glare, she replied, 'Oh, we're used to it.' Clearly, the Queen Mother regards media coverage as more than an intrusion or just an inevitable part of the job. She treats the camera as she does the bouquet, the plaque or the visitors' book: as a necessary and vital part of the ceremony.

I compare notes with Nick, a friend who shares my interest in photography, but whose sole subject matter is mountains. As I have pointed out, he does not face the problem of another mountain getting in the way at the last minute, or a mountain suddenly driving off. Fortunately, it is impossible here to record in detail some of the other problems, such as the acute agony of the photographer under pressure from a migraine, sunstroke, a full bladder, or rain-drenched clothes. There is also the constant threat of old ladies asking you how to mend their cameras. Then there is the other terror – the over-helpful local, the know-it-all who sends photographers on an imaginary shortcut down a towpath that finishes up with the irate cameraman on one side of a river and the royal visit on the other.

THE ANNUAL ROUND

The Queen Mother's year, like the Queen's, follows a rigid pattern of public and private tradition. The Christmas season is usually spent at Windsor and Sandringham, Easter at Windsor, the late summer and autumn in Scotland. Two annual visits to the UK by foreign heads of state; the Season (including the Derby, Trooping the Colour and Royal Ascot) and Remembrance Sunday are set dates in the Queen Mother's calendar.

Outside this formal structure, each member of the Royal Family has his or her own pattern of engagements. The Queen Mother's year includes the now traditional visit to Chelsea Barracks on 17 March – St Patrick's Day – to present shamrock to the Irish Guards. There is also a visit each July to one or more of the Cinque Ports, of which she is Lord Warden. Soon afterwards she attends a service for the Friends of St Paul's Cathedral. Also in the summer, she makes her annual visit to selected areas of the capital as part of the London Gardens Scheme, to the Sandringham Flower Show and to the King's Lynn Festival. In August there is her usual birthday appearance outside Clarence House, and in September the visit to the Braemar Games. Her return from Scotland is timed to precede the service at St Margaret's Church, Westminster, where she presents her own poppy on the Thursday before Remembrance Sunday. Finally, in December, there are her traditional visits to the Royal Smithfield Show and the Royal College of Music.

Interspersed with these appearances are individual engagements, mainly located in London but also scattered throughout the UK (1988 alone saw visits to Glasgow, Cambridge, Birmingham, Egham, Goring-on-Thames, Saffron Walden, Newcastle, Cardiff, Doncaster, Hitchin, Norwich and Warwick). Added to these are private visits to the races – Newbury, Cheltenham, Sandown Park and Kempton – a spring holiday on the Continent (Sicily in 1988), two breaks in the Scottish Highlands and several visits to friends throughout the country.

This seems a gruelling routine, yet, far from flagging, the Queen Mother undertook fifteen more engagements in 1988 than in the previous year and has a list of invitations that will take her well into the 1990s.

WHAT IS SHE REALLY LIKE?

Mention the Queen Mother to anyone and you can guarantee that they will ask, 'Is she really always so nice?' Having photographed the Queen Mother on all but a few of her 1988-9 engagements, I am fervently and unequivocally won over by her. Perhaps the best way I can answer the question is by describing the image that I have seen the Queen Mother present on both public and private engagements.

Queen Elizabeth obviously derives great fulfilment from making public appearances. Even the most routine engagement finds her in high spirits. Yet this mood is tempered by the formality that surrounds her and the high standards that she insists on. Her staff, whether leaving a room or climbing out of a car, always have to face her, and even on private occasions her family arrives to visit her in order of precedence, and each one, apart from the Queen, will bow and curtsy to her.

She is a natural and very gracious flirt, and produces in men a chivalry that recalls a romantic, bygone era. Also, she has a romantic's love of flowers and much prefers the public's home-grown bunches, held together by tin foil and ribbon, to an official bouquet. She dislikes plastic flowers, although these are preferable to those offered by 'Silly Sally' – a Brixton woman in her sixties who continually tries to give the Royal Family photocopies of flowers. (I once heard an official say to Princess Margaret, 'Your Royal Highness, this lady wants to give you some flowers.' The Princess, recognizing another printed bunch, said, 'No way,' and shot into her waiting car.)

Children can be a menace with flowers, and many a distraught parent has seen £10 go down the drain when the youngster gives the bouquet to a mayoress or lady-in-waiting by mistake. In January 1988, when the Queen and Queen Mother were about to leave West Newton Church, near the Sandringham estate, a stream of small children were paired off to approach the royal ladies with flowers. A woman next to me in the crowd kept saying, 'Annabel, give them to the Queen, don't forget . . . the Queen.' As luck would have it, when Annabel's turn came, she faced the Queen Mother, gave her the flowers and then asked loudly, 'Are you the Queen?' The Queen Mother, slightly taken aback, said, 'Well no, it's my daughter . . .' and indicated the present monarch. Obviously bearing in mind her mother's instructions, Annabel grabbed back the flowers and gave them to the Queen, who turned round with a deadpan expression and said, 'Got it right that time!'

Romance is also evoked by the Queen Mother's style: the reassuringly familar silk or velvet coat, the matching soft-brimmed hat, the pearls, the brooch and the teetering 3½-inch heels, which, in the 1920s, forced several city authorities temporarily to fill in their tram-lines for her visit. Although the style may vary little, the colours embrace a whole spectrum of blues, greens, pinks and yellows, and no matter where in the UK I have travelled to photograph the Queen Mother, the guessing game of 'What will she wear?' is usually played somewhere among the well-wishers.

Excited voices vie in the race to spot the chosen shade, and there is often confusion when the Queen Mother is barely visible on the horizon. 'Oh, she's in lime green,' yelled sixty-three-year-old Edna Daley from Norwich, who had somehow confused Her Majesty with one of the helicopter landing crew at the city's airport. Another myopic senior citizen, Harold Greenaway, insisted that the Queen Mother had chosen a navy-blue two-piece for her visit to Glasgow, when his view of the royal guest had in fact been obscured by a policewoman.

For the many people who meet royalty only once in a lifetime, the experience can be thrilling. The Queen Mother is not only aware of the significance of each new introduction, but clearly thrives on this centre-stage role, needing the public as much as the public love and respect her. I remember fifty-three-year-old George Aldred telling the Queen Mother that he had fulfilled a lifetime's ambition when he met her at Saffron Walden in July. She replied, 'Well, I'm so glad that we've met now,' as if she too had waited half a century for the meeting. It is the same throughout the country. In Birmingham, a taxi driver deserted his cab to watch her pass by. He kept repeating, 'She's the greatest,' as tears poured down his face.

The Queen Mother herself is thrilled by the meetings, particularly when people such as eighty-six-year-old Alice Maynard from Ely, confused with excitement, tell her, 'You're one of my greatest admirers.' A two-way process is evolved: the crowd is made to feel important and to feel relevant to the success of the engagement.

I have overheard her ask the inevitable royal question, 'Where do you come from?' and after receiving the usual reply, 'Hampstead', 'Twickenham', 'Leeds', she always follows it with the delighted exclamation 'Oh, Hampstead . . .' as if she knows the place well. I even heard 'Oh, Missouri!' when she visited Egham. Similarly, when she is driving past a crowd, she selects particular people to smile at and acknowledge in order to make them feel special.

Consider this aptitude for public relations in its wider context, and it is possible to argue that the Queen Mother has done a lot to democratize the Royal

Family. She is after all the first commoner to have married a future King of England since Anne Hyde married James, brother of Charles II, when, like King George VI, he himself was Duke of York. With King George, the Queen Mother developed the Royal Family's ability to associate itself successfully with ordinary men and women, mainly owing to the temporary levelling of classes that occurred during the war. Their visits to badly bombed areas set the precedent for royal visits to the scenes of disasters, such as the Queen's visit to Aberfan in 1966 and that of the Prince and Princess of Wales to Enniskillen in 1987.

It is amazing how many times, even today, the war comes up in conversation during the Queen Mother's engagements around the country. When she visited the Manor Gardens Community Centre in North London, she talked about rationing and the price of butter with ninety-four-year-old Kitty Gregg. In July she met the last remaining 'Old Contemptibles' at Chelsea Hospital, and in the same month, during her visit to Brixton, she saw the Anderson shelter in the back garden of Elsie and George Spragg's house. In Walmer I heard her say to eighty-three-year-old Alf Morris, 'We never knew what Hitler was going to do next, did we?' At Winchester two years earlier she greeted a line-up of elderly WAFs with the delightful comment 'Thank you for helping to save England', and during a tour of Bermondsey she met Lillian Collins, who was thirteen when the Queen Mother sent her family a food parcel after the Blitz.

This process of democratization can also be seen in the Queen Mother's attempts to integrate the Royal Family into the local community near each of the royal estates. For instance, at Balmoral she and the Queen attend the biennial sale of works at Crathie Church, and at Sandringham they have tea with the local Women's Institute. In January 1988 both sent jugs from the royal collection to be included in a Women's Institute display and custard tarts from the Sandringham kitchens for a competition on the same day. It was amusing to overhear the Queen Mother ask, 'Was the custard all right?' and it was just as much fun to see her success in the garden-produce competition at the Royal Windsor Flower Show:

Best Spring Onions – 1st Prize: HM Queen Elizabeth the Queen Mother.
Best Carrots – 1st Prize: HM Queen Elizabeth the Queen Mother.
Best Peas – Disqualified: HM Queen Elizabeth the Queen Mother (only 8 not 10 on a plate).

Obviously someone had decided to help themselves to a souvenir!

One of the most notable aspects of the Queen Mother's engagements is that whenever she visits a town or city, diligent officials always seem to have scoured the district for someone the same age as Her Majesty to present to her. Unfortunately, many of these near-nonagenarians do not share the Queen Mother's robust state of health, and it must be very dispiriting for her to meet a wheelchair-bound old dear and to be told, 'Mrs Sedgeman is exactly the same age as Your Majesty!' Happily, the Queen Mother seems to take it all in her stride, to the extent of her straightening the blanket covering eighty-nine-year-old Gertrude Nelson's knees at the Windsor Flower Show in July 1988, saying, 'Now do keep warm, won't you?' When, a month earlier, Her Majesty met eighty-six-year-old Mrs Emily Silverside in Newcastle, the latter told her, 'We're all travelling on,' to which the Queen Mother replied, 'Yes, we are, aren't we,' before hurrying off to open a leisure park and then flying back to Heathrow in time for a dinner engagement in London.

If it is a case of survival of the fittest, the Queen Mother definitely has the last word. As I photographed her at a reception at Norwich Airport, the city's former mayor, Ted Gambling, told her, 'We're a couple of oldsters. I'm eighty-four.' 'Yes,' said the Queen Mother, wagging her finger, 'but I can beat you!'

The democratizing role of the Queen Mother also influences her leisure activities, especially national hunt racing, which brings her in touch with race-goers from all social backgrounds. Her visits to the races are part of the same annual pattern as many of her public engagements. In this way, her yearly call at grocer Philip Delaney's shop in Prestbury, on her way to the Cheltenham Gold Cup, has itself become one of the traditions on which the Queen Mother bases her style of royalty.

Should an important race coincide with a public engagement, the Queen Mother will, if the timing permits, listen to the live broadcast over the car radio. I remember several years ago waiting anxiously as she took ten minutes to alight from her Rolls-Royce after returning to Clarence House. A member of the household later confirmed that, far from having been taken ill as I had feared, the Queen Mother, with her entourage, had stayed in the drive to listen to the 4.15 at Newmarket.

The Queen Mother is very much at ease in the predominantly male environment of the racecourse, and many of her other social activities revolve around the company of men. Some of her friends are company directors in the City, and she lunches with them, as well as with the various regiments of which she is Colonel-in-Chief and with dons, particularly in Oxford. Before entertaining her at Merton College, her hosts checked with Clarence House to determine what refreshments should accompany the lunch. An official replied that Malvern water would be appreciated. This was misinterpreted at the Oxford end of the phone-line as an ironic request for 'more than water'. As a result, the Queen Mother was offered every type of alcoholic delight.

The world is her oyster, yet many of the Queen Mother's recreational activities are modest. While staying at the Castle of Mey, she makes excursions to art galleries in Thurso, and during her summer visits to Sandringham attends exhibitions and concerts at King's Lynn. There are visits to the theatre, and the more contemplative pursuits of gardening and reading poetry. Her devotion to her corgis is renowned, and after last year's Trooping the Colour, I photographed her leaving Clarence House for Windsor only to see her return minutes later roaring with laughter, since in her hurry she had forgotten to take the corgis.

All of these private pursuits are to some degree a security risk, requiring an increase in the size of the Royalty Protection force and in the number of police guarding the royal palaces. The Queen Mother treats the officers with the same personal consideration that characterizes much of her contact with the public. A WPC who was seconded to work at Buckingham Palace told me that on her first day on duty there, a radio signal warned her to open the ten-foot-high gates at the garden entrance to the palace, as the Queen Mother was about to leave for Clarence House after dining with the Queen. As the policewoman pushed the gates back, one side became jammed by gravel from the forecourt. Fortunately, a voice said, 'Do you think I can help you?' and the policewoman was amazed to see the Queen Mother, then well over eighty, get out of her car and try very gently to push the gates open.

LOOKING BACK

How do I feel after this year-long pursuit? Well, it has been rewarding, exhausting, fascinating, and above all it has been fun. I knew in the spring of 1988 when I cycled at eleven at night through thick fog and absolute blackness, on the eight miles from King's Lynn to a bed-and-breakfast farm near the royal estate at Sandringham, that the year would either make or break me. Seven thousand miles and 300 films later, I can relax and look back on a year packed with unforgettable experiences. There was my first visit to a racecourse (Sandown Park), in March, and my first bet (£6 'either way' on the Queen Mother's Lunedale, which romped home in the 2.15 to win its owner £3,500 – and me a good deal less).

There was the parade at Windsor in May when the Queen Mother pointed and waved across to the photographers she recognized. The same month there was her visit to the Royal Holloway and Bedford New College at Egham. When she passed by, I asked her how she was liking the flat season and she said, 'Well it's rather difficult, but I'm learning to cope.' It was there, too, that several students, protesting against cuts in their grants, booed Her Majesty's arrival at the Students' Union, while the photographers put down their cameras to cheer her.

At the beginning of June, the Queen Mother opened the police convalescence home at Goring-on-Thames. I attended a champagne reception with 300 policemen who, finding it difficult to relax off duty, looked at me suspiciously – like a team of undertakers reviewing a prospective client. A week later there was the royal visit to Carver Barracks, near Saffron Walden, when I managed to hitch a lift with a senior officer who only the day before had had another VIP visit from 'the director of Star Wars'. I nervously twittered, 'Steven Spielberg's brilliant, isn't he?' only to be crushed by the reply, 'As a matter of fact, it was General Abrahamson.'

That same afternoon, the Queen Mother attended a fête in a disused hangar in the grounds of the barracks. Everyone moved back to give Her Majesty an unimpeded view of an inflated 'fun castle' that was being pummelled by hundreds of tiny feet. As she laughingly pointed at them, a small boy ran forward, put 10p in her hand, and jumped on the castle.

On 4 August, I and four other photographers went on a mad taxi chase round London's West End in a desperate bid to locate the theatre that the Queen Mother was visiting for a birthday treat. We succeeded with seconds to spare.

Finally, in October, there was another breakneck journey through the traffic to get to the VIP entrance at Heathrow in time for the Queen Mother's return from Scotland. Here, I unwittingly caused a temporary strike among the airport photographers, who objected to my being allowed to photograph the arrival from the tarmac whereas they had been roped off behind barriers further away.

Photographing, over the course of a year, more than two thirds of the Queen Mother's engagements certainly gave me a unique view of a royal year. During the twelve months, I photographed Her Majesty arriving at fourteen church services without ever being allowed myself to sing a hymn or hear a sermon. In eight theatre visits I never saw a play, and at four concerts did not hear a note. I must be the only person to have travelled 100 miles to the Derby and not seen the race, and during my four days at Royal Ascot I swear I never saw a racehorse.

Throughout it all, being a born pessimist, I had to allow enough time to worry and to live through each engagement fifty times before it had even occurred. The only brief glimmer of hope was the knowledge that if I completely blew the next one, there would be 119 other chances to improve on it.

The Queen Mother was born during the reign of Queen Victoria. She has known four of Victoria's children, and she has lived to see Victoria's great-great-granddaughter reign for nearly forty years. She was Britain's last Empress of India and as a child she dined with Lord Rosebery. She was born during the Boer War and as Queen Consort served the British people through the gravest international conflict of the twentieth century, with the charm and dedication that apparently provoked Hitler into calling her 'the most dangerous woman in Europe'.

The Queen Mother still serves the country with charm and dedication. To her, the British people are fundamentally the same as they were during the war years, and she has adapted to the changing times with characteristic enthusiasm. She is a vital link with the past, embodying many of the virtues of earlier generations, yet remaining forward-looking and forward-thinking. She looks continually to the future, choosing for an eighty-fifth birthday treat a flight on Concorde, and at eighty-seven excitedly visiting Berlin for the first time, since when she has said that she cannot wait to return.

In compiling this book I have photographed the Queen Mother on every possible occasion since the beginning of 1988. During this time she has never missed an engagement, even though there must have been days when she did not feel up to appearing. What is still more impressive is that during this time she left earlier than planned on only one occasion. This surely is a record that few other members of the Royal Family can equal.

I remember as a child being unable to understand growing old. The elderly had lived for ever, and would go on living for ever, and the young, like me, would eventually do the same. Later, I learned to smile at such naivety, but today, seeing the Queen Mother living life to the full as she approaches her ninetieth birthday, it is hard not to believe as I once did.

March

At Chelsea Barracks.

Thursday 3rd
MANOR GARDENS

The Queen Mother visits the Manor Gardens Community Centre, Holloway, London.

TOP: It is exactly 60 years since her first visit, but the smile, the grace and the elegance are the same.
BOTTOM: A small crowd has waited for over two hours in intermittent rain and freezing temperatures. They are not disappointed: the Queen Mother talks to each person – and even the police join in the fun.

Wednesday 9th
GLASGOW

The Queen Mother visits Glasgow.

Naturally at home among the Scots, the Queen Mother shares many of their memories. Some people in the crowd had seen King George VI and Queen Elizabeth board the Vanguard *bound for South Africa in 1947, and three old ladies showed me a wartime beret clearly inscribed 'as worn by Princess Margaret Rose'.*
INSET: Arriving to open the £16-million Royal Scottish Academy of Music and Drama. At the time, news was filtering through of an official letter of inquiry concerning the closure of St Tydfil's Hospital in South Wales. Later, the Queen Mother was seen to wipe away a tear as the Academy choir sang 'Will ye no come back again', prompting one onlooker to complain, 'She might not have the chance if they close them down at this rate.'

LEFT: 'Are those for me? How very kind.' Nine hours after the Queen Mother's departure from Clarence House, another working day is over, and one little girl's dream has come true.
BELOW: The Queen Mother left Scotland half an hour later than planned. Outside the Academy, a shy little girl called Emma waits patiently to offer some flowers.

Saturday 12th
SANDOWN
PARK

The Queen Mother attends the Grand Military Meeting.

Standing in the members' enclosure at the entrance to the paddock.

LEFT: Lunedale, the Queen Mother's own hurdler and the 4–1 favourite, won the 2.15 race by several lengths. The proud owner congratulates the horse and its trainer.

BELOW: Stepping forward to receive the prize of £3,373.

Thursday 17th
CHELSEA
BARRACKS

The Queen Mother presents shamrock to the Irish Guards for St Patrick's Day.

Posing for the official photograph with the Colonel of the regiment, the Grand Duke of Luxembourg, on her right, and the Commanding Officer, Lt-Col Wilson, on her left. Since the Queen Mother never wears a uniform, she has chosen instead an outfit that exactly matches the shade of blue on the regimental plumes.

RIGHT: Reviewing a parade of the regiment's veterans after the main ceremony.

Monday 21st
THEATRE ROYAL, WINDSOR

The Queen Mother attends a performance of Dear Octopus *to mark the Golden Jubilee of the theatre company.*

She is greeted by the Lord Lieutenant of Berkshire. Theatre personnel had spent 20 minutes trying to arrange a red carpet that was six feet too short and therefore impossible to anchor over the pavement edge. As Her Majesty approached, the carpet began to roll forward with each step she took; fortunately, she neatly surfed over the rising wave, and disaster was averted.

Thursday 24th
ST MARY'S, PADDINGTON

The Queen Mother opens the new wing at St Mary's Hospital, Paddington.

Fifty-seven years after her first visit, she is greeted by the Lord Mayor of Westminster, Cllr Kevin Gardner. A few minutes earlier, the police band in the background had mistakenly struck up the welcoming melody when a taxi tried to park in the space reserved for Her Majesty's car.

Tuesday 29th
SANDOWN PARK

The Queen Mother attends the Royal Artillery Meeting.

BELOW: Heavy rain fails to deter her from entering the paddock to view the runners for the 2.00 race.
RIGHT: At ease with the racing fraternity, she prepares to leave the paddock after studying the form of the hurdlers in the main race, the 3.00 Gold Cup.

*Presenting the Royal Artillery Gold
Cup after the 3.00 race.*

*U*NVEILING PLAQUES *is a necessary hazard for any royal visitor. In the year 1988/9, the Queen Mother faced an intriguing array of designs, sizes and locations.*

At Walmer, Kent, the plaque was sited outside the church (June).

TOP ROW: How it should be done: a simple, straightforward speech; a quick glance at the plaque; and a smile for the photographers.
LEFT: At Rotherhithe, the Queen Mother helped with the cementing before the plaque was put into place in the living room of a 'self-built' house (July).

April

Leaving Downing College,
Cambridge.

Sunday 3rd
ST GEORGE'S, WINDSOR

The Queen Mother and other members of the Royal Family attend the Easter morning service at St George's Chapel, Windsor.

RIGHT: With the Dean (the Right Rev. Michael Mann), the Duke and Duchess of York and Mrs Mann, watching the Queen and Prince Philip leave the chapel on their way back to Windsor Castle.
BELOW: With typical consideration, she acknowledges visitors to the castle by waving to them from the private apartments.

Monday 11th
CAMBRIDGE

The Queen Mother visits the National Arts Collections Fund exhibition at the Fitzwilliam Museum.

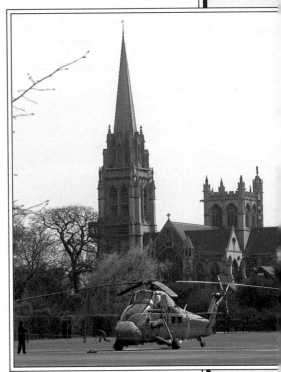

LEFT: Michael Jaffé, Director of the museum, retrieves a bunch of carnations that have fallen from the huge collection carried by the Queen Mother. She said to the girl who had presented them, 'I mustn't forget the precious one!'
ABOVE: The Wessex helicopter of the Queen's Flight lands at Downing College.

Thursday 21st
ST GEORGE'S, HANOVER SQUARE

The Queen Mother attends a concert in St George's Church, Hanover Square, given to mark the 250th anniversary of the Royal Society of Musicians of Great Britain.

In her capacity as patron of the Royal Society of Musicians, she arrives for a performance by the London Handel Choir and Orchestra.

RIGHT: 'Queen's-eye view': in her element at the races.
BELOW: In the winners' enclosure. The Queen Mother traditionally presents the prizes to the winning owner, trainer and jockey after the Gold Cup race.

Saturday 23rd SANDOWN PARK

The Queen Mother attends the Whitbread Gold Cup.

The winners' enclosure.

Tuesday 26th
LONDON SCOTTISH HEAD-QUARTERS

The Queen Mother opens the new regimental headquarters of the London Scottish in Horseferry Road, Westminster.

In her role as the regiment's Honorary Colonel.

Saturday 30th
BIRMINGHAM

*The Queen Mother visits the
Birmingham Botanical
Gardens.*

*Escorted by the Chairman of
the gardens, Michael Worley,
she opens the new £1.8-
million developments,
including a glasshouse
complex.*

*L*IKE THE UNVEILING *of the commemorative plaque, the signing of the visitors' book is a vital part of any royal engagement; these two procedures remain, in years to come, the main tangible moments of a royal visit. The Queen Mother's signature is as bold and firm as ever.*

Cardiff (July).

Cardiff (July).

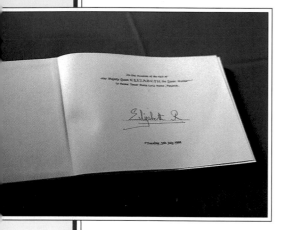

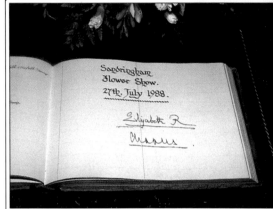

LEFT: 'Do you know the date?' Norwich (July). BELOW: Sandringham (July).

After a private luncheon in the City of London (December).

May

*At Windsor, an anxious look
at the sky before the parade
begins. Fortunately, the rain
held off.*

Tuesday 3rd
ST MARY-LE-BOW

The Queen Mother attends a service at St Mary-le-Bow Church in Cheapside, London, to mark its 900th anniversary.

RIGHT: Laughter in the sunshine as the Archbishop of Canterbury and a Pearly Queen wait to greet the guest of honour.
BELOW: Arriving at the church, looking radiant in sapphire blue.

Friday 6th
EGHAM

*The Queen Mother visits the
Royal Holloway and
Bedford New College,
Egham.*

*Arriving at the North Tower
of the college at 3.00 p.m. in
brilliant sunshine. The
college is part of the
University of London, of
which the Queen Mother is a
former Chancellor.*

Arriving at the Students' Union, accompanied by the Principal, Professor Dorothy Wedderburn. Several students, demonstrating against education cuts, booed the Queen Mother's arrival. Although she continued to smile, the hand on her pearls betrays a certain amount of insecurity. Later she asked for details of the students' grievances.

LEFT: *Dwarfed by the stone steps that lead down to the Founder's Quadrangle, she prepares to meet staff and students gathered in the gardens. One of her personal detectives, Inspector Dunn, surveys the scene, and behind him Ruth, Lady Fermoy is escorted by the two vice-principals.*
BELOW: *Having arrived on time, the Queen Mother immediately throws the programme awry by deciding on an impromptu walkabout among the students.*

Monday 9th
WINDSOR

The Queen Mother attends the parade in Windsor to mark the 20th anniversary of the granting of the Freedom of the Borough to the Brigade of Guards.

ABOVE: After lunch at the Guildhall, the Lord Lieutenant of Berkshire, Colonel Palmer, says farewell to the Queen Mother before she leaves for Royal Lodge.
RIGHT: The Irish Guards march along the High Street, past the dais. The Queen Mother's standard flies beneath the castle ramparts, and in the background Queen Victoria gloomily surveys the scene.

Tuesday 24th
FISHMONGERS HALL, LONDON

Patron of the National Trust for Scotland, the Queen Mother attends a concert of music found at Castle Fraser.

Thursday 26th
WESTMINSTER ABBEY

The Queen Mother attends a service to mark the Golden Jubilee of the Women's Royal Voluntary Service.

BELOW: The Duchess of Gloucester.
RIGHT: Partially obscured, the Queen Mother typically takes a step backwards in order to be visible to the photographers.

As the Queen Mother steps into her Rolls-Royce, one four-year-old seems to be more interested in the car than in its occupant.

Tuesday 31st
BARBICAN CENTRE, LONDON

The Queen Mother attends the opening performance of Les Arts Florissants.

Charming and elegant in a turquoise silk evening dress. The simplicity of the design helps to offset the intricate diamond-and-pearl necklace and the diamond earrings.

THE QUEEN MOTHER's household at Clarence House includes the Lord Chamberlain, the Comptroller, a private secretary and a press secretary, the treasurer, and a number of ladies-in-waiting – often personal friends – and equerries. Many of them have been with her for over thirty years.

With one of her personal detectives, Superintendent John Kirchin, and her steward, William Tallon, at Clarence House (August).

RIGHT: Followed by personal detective Inspector Dunn, in Egham (May).
BELOW: Superintendent Kirchin with the Queen Mother's press officer, Major John Griffin CVO, at Clarence House (August).

TOP: With lady-in-waiting Lady Elizabeth Bassett CVO, in Cambridge (April).
BOTTOM: The Queen Mother's private secretary, Lt-Col Sir Martin Gilliat GCVO, MBE, at the Middle Temple (December).

BELOW: Followed by her treasurer, Major Sir Ralph Anstruther Bt, at Sandringham (July).

RIGHT: With lady-in-waiting Lady Angela Oswald, at Sandown Park (March).

June

*At the opening of Flint House in Goring-on-Thames.
The photograph was taken as Lord Charteris, Chairman of
the appeal and former private secretary to the Queen,
mentioned that the Queen Mother's visit on such a dull,
overcast day occurred exactly 35 years after the Coronation,
when, at precisely the same time in the afternoon, heavy
rain had lashed the capital.*

BELOW: Boarding the royal train at Victoria Station.
BOTTOM LEFT: Three hours later, and wearing a different coat, the Queen Mother studies the form of the runners.

Wednesday 1st
DERBY

The Queen Mother and other members of the Royal Family attend the Derby.

LEFT: The Royal Family in the paddock before the race.
BELOW: Prince Philip.
RIGHT: Prince and Princess Michael of Kent.

Thursday 2nd
GORING-ON-THAMES

The Queen Mother opens Flint House, the Police Convalescence and Rehabilitation Trust home set up to provide accommodation for officers suffering from physical injury or the effects of stress.

At the garden party after the opening.

On being presented with a bench inscribed 'From Flint House', the Queen Mother asked the press, 'Do you want me to sit on it?' before posing for several shots. She decided that it would be 'ideal for Royal Lodge'.

Friday 10th
CARVER BARRACKS, SAFFRON WALDEN

The Queen Mother, Colonel-in-Chief, visits the 9th/12th Royal Lancers (Prince of Wales's) Regiment.

LEFT: Torrential rain threatened to mar the ceremony; the Queen Mother's scheduled arrival by helicopter was abandoned and she travelled from London by car.
RIGHT: Looking elegant in spite of the rain, wearing a cape to protect her coat and dress.
FAR RIGHT, TOP: The Queen Mother is older than all the retired soldiers on parade. For those who have travelled the length of the country to meet their Colonel-in-Chief again, it is an emotional moment.
FAR RIGHT, BOTTOM: The regimental band plays during the parade.

Saturday 11th
HORSE GUARDS PARADE

The Queen Mother attends Trooping the Colour in honour of the Queen's official birthday.

BELOW: The Queen on her way to Horse Guards Parade to review the Household Division. Both she and the Queen Mother have attended every one of the 36 troopings that have taken place since the Queen's accession in 1952.

RIGHT: With the Princess of Wales, passing Clarence House on the return journey to Buckingham Palace after the ceremony. The Queen Mother has noticed members of her staff watching the carriage procession.

RIGHT: The traditional balcony appearance after the ceremony. King Hussein of Jordan stands behind the Princess of Wales.

Monday 13th
ST GEORGE'S, WINDSOR

The Queen Mother attends the Garter service at St George's Chapel, Windsor.

ABOVE: In her role as Lady of the Garter, in the procession to the chapel.
RIGHT: With the Duke of Kent, on the return journey to Windsor Castle.

Resplendent in the Garter robes. The image is both formal and very feminine, and superbly complements her personal style. The Queen and Prince Philip were both created members of the Order of the Garter on St George's Day 1948, the 600th anniversary of the inauguration of the order.

Tuesday 14th – Friday 17th ASCOT

The Queen Mother attends Royal Ascot.

The Royal Family in the annual carriage procession from Windsor Great Park to Ascot Heath.
TOP: The Queen Mother and the Princess of Wales on the first day.
BOTTOM LEFT: The Queen Mother on the first day.
BOTTOM RIGHT: The Princess of Wales on the first day.

73

RIGHT: *The Queen Mother
and the Princess of Wales on
the second day.*
BELOW: *Princess Margaret
on the second day.*

LEFT: *The Queen Mother
on the third day.*
RIGHT: *The Queen on the
fourth and final day.*

Thursday 28th – Friday 29th TYNESIDE

The Queen Mother visits Tyneside.

LEFT & BELOW: Arriving at the Tyne Riverside Park, Newburn, accompanied by Sir Ralph Carr-Ellison, the Lord Lieutenant for Tyne and Wear. Behind them are Lady Grimthorpe, Lt-Col Sir Martin Gilliat and Captain Giles Bassett (respectively the Queen Mother's lady-in-waiting, private secretary and equerry).

RIGHT: In response to cheers from the crowd, she makes an impromptu appearance on a terrace above the new leisure centre. In spite of having attended more than half a dozen engagements in Tyneside, spread over two days, she looks relaxed and happy and is clearly thriving on seeing as many people as possible.

Receiving a painting of the Riverside Park. Always attentive and always sincere, she reacts as if this is the very gift she has always wanted.

FLOWERS

*T*HE QUEEN MOTHER *adores flowers, which is fortunate, since the public life of all the royal ladies inevitably revolves around them. She prefers the home-grown variety, wrapped in tin foil and lovingly presented, to any offical bouquet, and it is these that stand the greater chance of finishing the day on her writing desk.*

Piccadilly, London (November).

LEFT: *Chelsea Barracks (March).*
RIGHT: *Sandringham (July).*
BELOW: *Walmer, Kent (July).*

RIGHT: Chelsea Barracks (March).
BELOW: Cambridge (April).

July

At Holme Tower, Penarth, a specialist centre for cancer sufferers, the Queen Mother
helped to generate an atmosphere of happiness and optimism in a way
that would have been impossible for any other well-meaning official to match.

Tuesday 5th
PENARTH

The Queen Mother visits the Marie Curie Memorial Foundation home at Holme Tower.

BELOW: At a garden party in the grounds.
RIGHT: Leaving the home – half an hour later than planned, having insisted on visiting all the patients, many of whom are terminally ill.

Friday 8th
WINCHELSEA

The Queen Mother, Lord Warden of the Cinque Ports, visits Winchelsea, East Sussex.

Walking through the ruined archway in the eastern section of St Thomas's Church. The church was never completed; it stands as a memorial to Winchelsea's prosperity before the devastation wrought by the Hundred Years War against France and the Black Death.

Sunday 10th
WALMER & ST MARGARET'S AT CLIFFE

The Queen Mother spends the morning at Walmer, and in the afternoon travels down the coast to St Margaret's at Cliffe, near Dover.

LEFT: Leaving St Margaret's with the Rev. Christopher Wayte, she jokes about the high step at the west door.

ABOVE: Wherever she is, whether in the UK or abroad, the Queen Mother always goes to a church service on Sunday. Here she attends Matins at St Mary's Church near Walmer Castle. BELOW: The memorial window in the Church of St Margaret's at Cliffe, which depicts the Zeebrugge ferry disaster and which the Queen Mother inspected later in the afternoon.

Wednesday 13th
ST PAUL'S CATHEDRAL

The Queen Mother attends the festival service of the Friends of St Paul's.

LEFT: Leaving the cathedral crypt after the service. Almost obscured by a line of choirboys, she stands on tiptoe to wave to the crowd.

Saturday 16th
WINDSOR

The Queen Mother attends the Royal Windsor Flower Show.

ABOVE & LEFT: Members of the RAF Halton gymnastic display team perform for Her Majesty.

ABOVE: Presenting the awards to royal estate workers during the course of the afternoon.
RIGHT: The ubiquitous soft-brimmed hat, the veil, the pearls and the inimitable smile.

Sunday 17th
ST PAUL'S WALDEN

The Queen Mother attends a church service at St Paul's Walden, Hertfordshire.

At the parish church. The Queen Mother had arrived in St Paul's Walden the previous evening to spend the weekend with her sister-in-law Lady Bowes-Lyon, widow of the Queen Mother's brother David.

Leaving the church after the service.

Sunday 17th
HITCHIN

The Queen Mother visits the Sue Ryder home at Stagenhoe, near Hitchin, Hertfordshire, which provides care for people suffering from the crippling disease Huntington's chorea.

LEFT: She spoke to nearly all the patients and made a special point of privately visiting those most severely affected.
BELOW: Presenting Lady Ryder with a signed copy of her 75th-birthday photograph taken by Norman Parkinson.

Tuesday 19th
BRIXTON

The Queen Mother visits Brixton as part of the London Gardens scheme.

RIGHT: Every July the Queen Mother visits a different London suburb, usually in the early evening. The visits are relaxed and as informal as possible, and each one usually takes her to at least five different venues.
BELOW: Like many members of the Royal Family, the Queen Mother makes a point of chatting to the elderly. Often, as in this case, the senior citizens are probably some 20 years younger than her.

LEFT: *This tour, perhaps more than any other, shows the Queen Mother's ability to involve herself in the heart of a community.*

BELOW: *Stopping at the home of Elsie and George Spragg, in Calais Street, to look at the garden and to visit their Anderson shelter, which she said was 'a thrill'.*

Thursday 21st
ROTHERHITHE

The Queen Mother visits the London Docklands Development programme at Surrey Docks – her first formal visit to the docks since the height of the Blitz.

LEFT: She visits the Surrey House Self-Build Project to meet a group of men who are constructing their own homes.

BELOW: The Queen Mother's Daimler stops outside the Blacksmiths Arms, where Her Majesty caused a hiccup in the official schedule by accepting an invitation from the landlord, Maxwell Leftwick, to step inside for a drink on the house. 'I think I would like to taste your beer,' she enthused, and chose a glass of Fuller's bitter.

ABOVE: Enthusiastic crowds line the royal route, which stretched several miles across the docklands.
LEFT: The Queen Mother makes a moving speech, recalling the enormous loss of life during World War II and the affection that she and the King felt for the East End, and expressing delight in the area's current rejuvenation.

Touched by the sight of the vast, impressive photographs of her wartime visits, she offered to pose for the photographers in front of the display.

Monday 25th
NORWICH

The Queen Mother opens the new developments at Norwich Airport.

LEFT: She receives the all-clear as she passes through a security search area.
BELOW: Presented with an enormous bouquet of flowers, she exclaims, 'These are very nearly as big as I am!'

*She boards her helicopter
bound for Sandringham,
having stayed for the
habitual half-hour longer
than planned.*

LEFT: Behind the Queen
Mother is her close friend the
Duchess of Grafton, Mistress
of the Robes to the Queen.
BELOW: The Queen Mother
is patron of the King's Lynn
Festival, which was founded
in 1950 by Ruth, Lady
Fermoy, the Queen Mother's
lady-in-waiting and the
grandmother of the Princess
of Wales.

Tuesday 26th
KING'S LYNN

The Queen Mother attends a
birthday concert given in her
honour at St Nicholas's
Church by the celebrated
cellist Mstislav
Rostropovich.

Wednesday 27th
SANDRINGHAM

The Queen Mother attends the 107th annual Sandringham Flower Show.

BELOW: Walking with her guests through Sandringham Park. Behind them in the distance is Sandringham Parish Church, where the Royal Family worship when they are in residence.

LEFT: *Sandringham House flying the Queen Mother's standard.*
BELOW: *The Prince of Wales, who, like his grandmother, appears naturally at ease talking to visitors to the show.*

*The Women's Institute stall
modestly advertises its raffle.*

*C*HARACTERISTICALLY THE QUEEN MOTHER'S *is the frank, exuberant expression that is sometimes mischievous, occasionally flirtatious, but always direct and totally sincere.*

Victoria, London (April).

TOP: Sandown Park (March).
BOTTOM: Clarence House (August).

LEFT: Chelsea Barracks
(March).
BELOW: Egham (May).

RIGHT: King's Lynn (July).
BELOW: Royal Courts of Justice, London (October).

August

Even on her birthday, the Queen Mother is always willing to pose for the camera.

Thursday 4th
LONDON

The Queen Mother celebrates her 88th birthday.

RIGHT: The first of several appearances is at 11 a.m., where she acknowledges the birthday salute as the guards of the Household Division play for her on their way to Buckingham Palace.

LEFT: *Dozens of children run forward with bunches of flowers, handmade cards and all kinds of presents.*
BELOW: *Three generations of the Royal Family join in the celebrations.*

The birthday treats continue as the Queen Mother arrives at the Theatre Royal, Haymarket, for a performance of J. M. Barrie's The Admirable Crichton *starring Rex Harrison.*

Sunday 13th
MEY

The Queen Mother attends the Highland Games in Mey, on the north coast of Scotland.

ABOVE: Range Rovers are not the easiest vehicles to climb out of with dignity. The Queen Mother, however, tries her best, assisted by the President of Canisbay Royal British Legion.
LEFT: Entering into the spirit of things.

Seated in a makeshift royal box – a plywood shelter with a tartan cloth pinned to it – the Queen Mother and her guests join in the excitement as her tug-of-war team wins the challenge cup. To the right of the box, Lt-Col Sir Martin Gilliat and private detective Inspector Dunn look well-dressed for eight weeks in the country.

Sunday 14th
SCRABSTER

The Queen Mother is reunited with the Queen and Prince Philip at Scrabster, further west along the coast near Thurso.

LEFT: The Queen's launch leaves the Royal Yacht Britannia on her way to the harbour.
BELOW: The Queen Mother affectionately greets her daughter and son-in-law. The reunion is to be brief: the Queen and Prince Philip will stay for lunch and afternoon tea before reboarding the yacht at 5.30 p.m.

*She waves her scarf until the
launch is out of sight behind
the harbour walls.*

PLANTING TREES

Few people can lay claim to have been planting trees since 1923. Since so many were damaged in the storms of October 1987, the Queen Mother must have found that business has been on the increase.

Goring-on-Thames (June).

RIGHT: Egham (May).
FAR RIGHT: Birmingham (April).
BELOW: Winchelsea (July).

September

The Royal Family arrives at the Princess Royal and Duke of Fife Memorial Park in Braemar. The procession is led by the Queen, Prince Philip and Prince Edward; the Queen Mother is accompanied by the Prince and Princess of Wales.

Saturday 3rd
BRAEMAR

The Queen Mother and other members of the Royal Family attend the Highland Games at the Braemar Gathering, Grampian, Scotland.

FAR LEFT: The royal cars progress at a walking pace to allow the 20,000 spectators an excellent view of the royal party.
LEFT: Massed pipe bands salute their patron, the Queen, and her family.

Sunday 4th
CRATHIE

The Queen Mother attends a service at the parish church in Crathie, near Balmoral, Grampian.

With the Queen on the way back from Crathie, where, whenever they have been in residence at Balmoral, generations of the Royal Family have worshipped on Sundays since 1848.

*E*ACH MEMBER OF *the Royal Family has his or her own coat of arms. The heraldic design on the Queen Mother's standard and warrant combines the four quarters of the royal arms with those of the Bowes-Lyon family.*

The Queen Mother's warrant,
Ballater, near Aberdeen (September).

LEFT: The Queen Mother's standard on the Lord Provost's car, Glasgow (March).
RIGHT: The royal cipher on the Ascot livery (June).

October

A regal descent at chilly Heathrow.

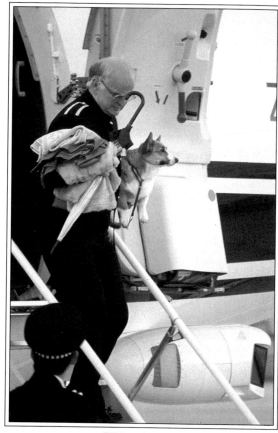

Wednesday 26th
HEATHROW

The Queen Mother returns from her ten-week holiday in Scotland.

ABOVE: Fortunately, she is not restricted to one piece of hand luggage on each flight. In fact, sometimes it's easier not to bother packing at all: here, her steward bravely struggles with a mink wrap, a coat, a towel, an umbrella and a coolly indifferent corgi.
RIGHT: A final word of thanks to airport staff.

Sunday 30th
STRAND, LONDON

The Queen Mother unveils a statue of Air Chief Marshal Lord Dowding opposite St Clement Danes Church.

ABOVE: After some initial difficulty locating the correct draw-string, she reveals the statue, which was paid for by former pilots and by public subscription. Earlier, Her Majesty had made a moving speech recalling Lord Dowding's outstanding qualities of leadership in the Battle of Britain.

*After the ceremony, she
attends a reception given by
the Battle of Britain Fighter
Association in the nearby
Royal Courts of Justice.*

*T*HE QUEEN MOTHER *exudes enthusiasm and* joie de vivre. *She does not merely take in information and witness events passively, but indicates exactly what it is that interests her. It is one of her ways of showing that she cares.*

Sandringham (July).

ABOVE: *Cardiff (July).*
RIGHT: *Sandringham (July).*
BELOW: *Egham (May).*

November

*Leaving Warwick, laden
with flowers.*

Tuesday 8th
WARWICK

The Queen Mother visits the historic Lord Leycester Hospital.

At 11.25 a.m. she arrives at the hospital's main entrance and is greeted by the Governors and their wives. INSET: The Queen Mother leaves the magnificent Tudor buildings accompanied by Viscount de Lisle, patron of the hospital's Governors, and Captain Lee, the Master of the hospital.

ABOVE: *The Queen Mother leaves the Great Hall of the hospital after signing the visitors' book.*
RIGHT: *After Her Majesty's afternoon visit to the George Marshall Centre, the resource centre for the Warwickshire Association for the Blind, hundreds of schoolchildren wait restlessly for her to walk past.*

Thursday 10th
ST MARGARET'S, WESTMINSTER

The Queen Mother visits the Field of Remembrance at St Margaret's Church.

ABOVE: The Queen Mother stands in silent tribute to the dead of two world wars. RIGHT: Later, in her more usual high spirits, she leaves the church, followed by her press secretary, Major John Griffin. The Queen Mother looks stunning in black, but chooses to wear it only at Remembrance services and for family mourning.

Thursday 10th
MERCHANT TAYLORS HALL, LONDON

The Queen Mother attends a reception given by the Royal Yeomanry.

An officer of the Royal Yeomanry salutes his Honorary Colonel as she goes off duty, nine hours after starting her day at St Margaret's Church.

Sunday 13th
THE CENOTAPH

The Queen Mother is present at the Remembrance Day ceremony at the Cenotaph in Whitehall.

RIGHT: On the balcony of the old Home Office building, the royal group pay homage to the nation's fallen. From left to right are King Olav of Norway, the Princess of Wales, Prince Edward, the Queen Mother and Princess Anne.
BELOW: Eyes right as the press prepare for the Royal Family's arrival.

Tuesday 15th
ROYAL FINE ART COMMISSION

The Queen Mother visits the Royal Fine Art Commission in St James's Square, London.

Her Majesty arrives for lunch, stepping demurely from her car into the square.

Monday 21st
LONDON PALLADIUM

The Queen Mother attends the Royal Variety Performance.

After being greeted by Lord Delfont, she goes up the steps to the entrance.

Tuesday 22nd
ROYAL HOSPITAL CHELSEA

The Queen Mother plants a tree in the grounds of the Royal Hospital Chelsea.

RIGHT: Rows of Chelsea pensioners welcome the royal visitor, who told them that they formed 'a lovely backdrop'.

FAR RIGHT, TOP: The Queen Mother moves along the ranks of elderly pensioners. It was a sobering thought to realize that she was the oldest person on parade.

FAR RIGHT, BOTTOM: She plants the first of 28 tulip trees that are to replace those damaged by the storms of October 1987.

Wednesday 23rd
BARBICAN CENTRE, LONDON

The Queen Mother attends the Royal Concert at the Barbican Hall.

She arrives for the concert, which is given in aid of the Musicians Benevolent Fund.

Tuesday 29th
WESTMINSTER ABBEY

The Queen Mother attends a memorial service for Sir Frederick Ashton.

After the service, she leaves the abbey with Princess Margaret.

Tuesday 29th
ROYAL COLLEGE OF MUSIC

The Queen Mother pays her annual visit to the Royal College of Music.

Her detective, Inspector Dunn, makes sure that her elegant lilac velvet coat and hat remain dry.

*I*NEVITABLY, *THE CAMERA'S split-second accuracy does not always produce the intended effect.*

The flash-unit that recharged too late
(Merchant Taylors Hall, November).

BELOW: *The overkeen official (Theatre Royal, London, August).*
RIGHT: *Making room for the dog (Chelsea Barracks, March).*

The sudden breeze (Walmer, July).

December

Few people can remain smiling when faced with 100 of the latest agricultural gadgets, but Her Majesty appears fascinated as the 101st is explained to her at the Royal Smithfield Show. Unlike the Queen Mother, none of the 50-odd photographers covering the visit ever found out what this one is supposed to be for!

Wednesday 7th
EARLS COURT

The Queen Mother visits the Royal Smithfield Show.

RIGHT: Looking more suitably equipped for a flower show, Her Majesty tours the meat-carcass section.

BELOW: The Queen Mother not only presented the prizes, but received one herself, for the winning Aberdeen Angus heifer – the only first prize that her cattle have won in 40 years of showing.

Thursday 8th
MIDDLE TEMPLE

The Queen Mother dines with the Benchers at the Middle Temple in London.

In spite of freezing temperatures, she deliberately pauses to enable the six of us taking photographs to get a good view.

Friday 17th
ST PAUL'S CATHEDRAL

The Queen Mother attends the London Fire Brigade's Christmas carol service.

After the service, she walks between the ranks of a line-up of London Fire Brigade officers on the steps of the cathedral.

AFTER ANY PUBLIC APPEARANCE, most people would want to sit back in the car and relax. The Queen Mother chooses to sit forward, to smile and occasionally to wave through the open window. She is not only making sure that everyone sees her, but showing how reluctant she is to go.

*Arriving back at Clarence House
after a concert (March).*

LEFT: *Cardiff (July).*
BELOW: *Rotherhithe (July).*

January

*The Queen leads her family to morning
service at Castle Rising Parish Church.*

Thursday 19th
SANDRINGHAM

The Queen Mother attends the monthly meeting of Sandringham Women's Institute.

BELOW: The Queen Mother, President of Sandringham Women's Institute, is met by the Vice-President.

Two hours later, the Queen Mother says goodbye to the committee members. The Queen, having waited several minutes for her mother to finish chatting, finally decided to go ahead alone and sit in the car.

Sunday 22nd
CASTLE RISING

The Queen Mother and other members of the Royal Family attend a service at Castle Rising Parish Church, near King's Lynn, Norfolk.

FAR LEFT: The Queen and the Queen Mother outside the church at Castle Rising. The Royal Family traditionally worship at Sandringham Parish Church on the royal estate on the first three Sundays of the year; on the fourth and sixth Sundays, the Queen attends a service at one of the local churches – West Newton, Dersingham, Flitcham, Hillington or Castle Rising.
ABOVE: The Royal Family are preceded by choristers and citizens of Castle Rising.

*Prince Andrew drives the
Duchess of York back to
Sandringham House after
the service.*

*T*HE DEFINITIVE ROYAL WAVE *is never too formal, never uncertain, but always friendly, graceful and genuine.*

Brixton (July).

FAR LEFT: Cambridge (July).
LEFT: Goring-on-Thames (June).
BELOW: St Paul's Cathedral (July).

Walmer (July).

February

*Acknowledging the crowd as she
leaves Westminster Abbey.*

Thursday 9th
WESTMINSTER ABBEY

The Queen Mother attends the Royal Air Force Benevolent Fund Trenchard memorial service.

BELOW LEFT: Her Majesty seems slightly concerned about walking over the medieval cobbles outside the Deanery.
BELOW RIGHT: As she enters the car, she slips forward on to the floor of the vehicle, losing her shoe in the process.

BELOW: *Mrs Patrick Campbell-Preston, the Queen Mother's lady-in-waiting, and the abbey's verger run forward to help her, and the shoe is retrieved; the Queen Mother was later to wave it out of the window as the car drove off.*

The Queen Mother's car with its outriders passes through Parliament Square.

Wednesday 15th
MANSION
HOUSE

*The Queen Mother attends a
reception at Mansion House
in the City of London.*

*Happy and glorious . . . She
leaves the reception later
than planned – as usual.*

I am indebted to Her Majesty Queen Elizabeth the Queen Mother's press officer, Major John Griffin CVO, and to his assistant, Mrs Lucy Murphy LVO, for their time and patience in answering many wide-ranging and often intricate questions, and for their encouragement since the project began in February 1988.

I am also grateful to the following friends for their constructive comments and support: Louisa Hardman, Alison Maclean, Eva Moore, Martine and Michael Stewart and Deborah Wood.

Finally I would like to thank my editors, David Reynolds and Penny Phillips at Bloomsbury, for their courage in taking on board an unknown author, and for their sound common sense.

Ian Lloyd

A percentage of the author's royalty earnings will be donated to a charity personally chosen by Her Majesty Queen Elizabeth the Queen Mother.

This project was partially sponsored by Kodak Limited. All the transparencies used were taken on Kodak Ektachrome.

June 90